SOME DAYS ARE SANDSTONE

poems

ABBY HARDING

Nodding Onion Press

Nodding Onion Press

P.O. Box 242
Hanna City, IL 61536
noddingonionpress.com

Copyright © 2024 by Abby Harding

All rights reserved, including the right to reproduce this book or portions thereof in any form without written permission from the author.

First hardcover edition October 2024

Cover designed using Canva.com.
Interior designed using Microsoft Word.
Interior font set in Perpetua.

ISBN 979-8-9913594-0-5

For A, B, C, and D.
You're my favorite alphabet.

Table of Contents

Foreword

Going Through the Motions 1

Geminids 3

Health Scare 4

Go Fish 7

Aurora Borealis 8

Three Evening Haikus 9

Mirror, mirror 10

Winter's End 12

Weathered 13

Burnout 14

Solar Eclipse 16

Waiting on Inspiration 17

Mommy, carry 18

Some Days Are Sandstone 19

April 12, 1998 20

Ticklish 22

Love Me Anyway 23

Good Intentions 24

Insecure 26

Things I don't let myself enjoy because I feel I
didn't earn them enough 27

Today we moved the chickens 28

Mother's Day 30

Social Anxiety 31

After the Phone Call 32

Blocked 34

Better than caffeine 35

Beach-wise 36

Ravenous 38

One marriage ends every 36 seconds 39

Demodex 40

Positive Reinforcement 42

Annoyance 45

PMS	46
Upon seeing my children's shoes on the floor	47
Be Water	49
Wednesday Evening, 7:34pm	50
Writing Sprint	51
Billy Collins Envy	52
News Cycle	53
Eldest Daughter Syndrome	54
This is a poem about overthinking	55
Directions	56
Lame Duck	58
How I hurt my own feelings today:	59
By the Creek	60
Small Talk	61
To the man I never write poetry for	62
Graffiti	63
Thing of Beauty	65
Closing House	66
Busy	68
Middle Ages	69
This is a poem about body image	70

Reliquary 71

Willms Road 73

Acknowledgements

Credits

About the Author

Foreword

Writing poetry
—I begin, mumbling my way
through an ephemeral maze—
just feels *right.*

The words piddle from my lips;
their hollow centers echo
the inexplicable.
But how do you describe the vibration
of recognizing your soul on a page,
of finding just the right phrase
       image
            sound
to capture a moment, distilled
—be it memory, emotion, or
simply the beauty-pain of living?

Words fail me, and I close my eyes, searching.
I press my hand to my chest, like I can reach in
and pluck out my heart, dripping ink,
to show you.

Going Through the Motions

Muddling through never felt so good.
Reading the same book again and again,
making routine love with your socks on,
as the laundry cheerfully molders
in cornered baskets, reeking of mediocrity.

Being self-aware only leads to hurt
—stubbing your toes on overflowing ashtrays
of bad habits and double-standards—
but in inevitable moments of crystallization
you know with frozen lungs
the only thing holding you together
is a tenuous attraction of atoms
your own personal Hiroshima waiting to happen
    (no way to know
    who you are
    at any given time).

It's the collapsing sensation
in the center of your body
when you wake to find
you're living someone else's life,
when you nearly lean over to kiss the wrong lips—

the inhale where you learn we are all
fish in a splintered mirror, countless refractions
of a thousand broken scales,
drowning in glass, choking on air.

Geminids

The first time I held your hand,
we sprawled under a winter sky
and stared at the stars,
marveling at their icy heat,
the gravity that holds them together.

"My fingers are cold,"
I whispered, sliding them between
your own strong hands,
excusing my presence.

You didn't seem to mind,
and I traced the imagined pattern of our
life on the palm of your hand—
shapes in the stars,
finding fortune and fate,
willing a story with you in it.

Health Scare

Hold your breath...

I didn't bring my phone or book,
nothing to fill the wait but racing thoughts.
What if it's something, not just a dimple in my skin
but a hitch in my life?

...and breathe.

I'm grateful the room is softly lit;
I'm grateful her hands are warm and dry;
I'm grateful they took me seriously;
I'm grateful we decided to check.

Hold your breath...

No family history,
but that's no guarantee.
I could be that new data point,
the vector my daughters have to chase.

...and breathe.

The waiting is the hardest part.
Shouldn't they be back by now?
    More images, they say, just to check,
    just to be sure.

Hold your breath…

It's probably nothing.
    I wonder if I'll have to do chemo.
I refuse to catastrophize with no information.
    I'm dying my hair purple before it all falls out.

…and breathe.

More waiting. I've been waiting for weeks.
This is their normal, their day job,
but I'm lost at sea,
trying not to wonder what lurks beneath my feet.

Hold your breath…

Two days before Christmas, I noticed it
    —has that always been there?
Now I mark every ache, every twinge,
unsure what normal feels like.

…and breathe.

The doctor wants a sonogram.
More waiting, but now I have a magazine.
"Use your china, don't save it for a special day!"
I'm going to use the fuck out of my favorite things.

Hold your breath...

One last dark room,
lying alone with my thoughts
then—all clear, just denser tissue.
        Come back when you're forty.

...and breathe.

I try to leave my fear in the stall
where I discard the robe,
but my body doesn't feel like home again yet,
the metallic taste of mortality lingering on my tongue.

Go Fish

we huddle around the table
hands tenderly cradling mugs of coffee
like the heads of our infants
while we swap our cards

>—Oh, you have two 'tantrums'
>   and a 'missed appointment'?
>—I'll give you my 'curdled cream' and
>   holographic 'diaper blowout' for your
>   deluxe 'three a.m. doom scroll'
>—My last pack only had two 'leaky breasts'
>   and 'forgotten laundry' in it
>—Have you seen the expansion set with
>   'spousal resentment' and
>   'broken water heater'?

we compare, find refuge in our similarities
all the while hoping someone
(who's willing to share)
has found 'releasing the weight of expectations'
and 'five minutes of uninterrupted silence'

Aurora Borealis

Usually, only the sight
of a blank page
silences me,
but tonight as I stare
gap-mouthed
at a view that should
elicit a psalter,
all I can do is
call the sky "intense"
as my limbs vibrate
with awe.

Three Evening Haikus

Geriatric cat
purring, pretzeled near my chair,
classic writing friend.

Within a hand's reach,
a honeyed mug of tea steams
chamomile and mint.

Rain on the window
drips cozy melancholy:
a perfect evening.

Mirror, mirror

We all know her:
she sighs into the phone
telling us how the pounds
slough off as she fights
an invisible battle with her body,
how frustrated she feels every time
a well-meaning friend-or-stranger
comments: how good
(how small, how thin, how narrow)
she looks these days.
She tells us she wishes
they wouldn't assume
she's losing weight on purpose,
how it hurts to hear,

then hours later
she posts a photo
of her shopping haul,
captioned something modest
about needing new clothes
because she's lost so much weight,

and we're angry,
not at the inconsistency
—though it rankles—
not even at Diet Culture
—though it sucks—
but at the way we see ourselves
reflected in her:
saying aloud,
again and again,
I will respect
my body at any size,
but quietly still believing
we'd be happier smaller.

Winter's End

It's not just the green
but the way joy is reaching out with tentative feelers
like a snail from its shell

Weathered

Today, the daffodils by the compost bin
finally raised their shy heads
and shed their green gowns,
trumpeting the return of spring.

Noting the battered, curling leaves,
reminders of a squall that sent the
tornado sirens into a tizzy,
I observed,
"They look a little worse for wear,"
conveniently ignoring my worry lines,
the dark circles under my eyes,
the way winter still hangs on my weary frame.

Burnout

We didn't notice at first
when our big male cat
began to drink too much water,

the first warning signs of his pancreas
slowing production,
letting the sugar build

and excrete in other ways.
We didn't notice, until
he started peeing blood

on our shoes.
I'm thirsty, too,
gluttonous for a shred

of myself to return,
taking deep swigs of solitude,
trying to find equilibrium

in a life that's sweet, but too full.
Hopefully, I'll notice the warning signs,
heed the crisp voice of intuition

before I start to bleed out
what's left of my sense
of self.

Solar Eclipse

The solar eclipse darkened our street today.
2 pm and cloudless, but I kept reaching to remove
the sunglasses I wasn't wearing. We craned

sunflower-faces as the world took on the cast
of early evening, but the shadows were all wrong
—unsettling curves and broken angles.

I wonder if the sun felt our eyes,
if she resented that we needed the moon to hide her
to marvel at her slow march across our sky,

as though she doesn't make the trip
to warm our skin and light the way
through a silent galaxy
every day of the year.

Waiting on Inspiration

I turn to the window and stare at the sky
hoping a star
or the silver toes of dusk
will light a fire in my imagination
and burn away the dregs of winter

I want to feel the keyboard
fish scale smooth
darting beneath my fingers
spelling out a spell
to explode the top of my head
as Dickinson said of poetry

But I am dumb
and numb
the words stillborn
on my tongue

Perhaps forcing a poem
only mimics art
like forcing a bulb
in a hot house
only mimics
the exuberance of spring

Mommy, carry

- ☐ My cup
- ☐ My jacket
- ☐ My blanket
- ☐ My endless energy
- ☐ My embarrassment
- ☐ My resentment
- ☐ My broken heart
- ☐ My terrifying human-ness
- ☐ My inherited traumas
- ☐ My fragility in a treacherous world
- ☐ Me

Some Days Are Sandstone

Some days are sandstone,
solid and unyielding,
but when met with water, wind,
and the slow drip of time,
they bend, melt into a shape
I don't recognize.

Today as I walked through the woods,
I wondered what shape this
solid
heavy
stone
of a day would yield
when met with a spring breeze
and the flow of icy winter melt
along the weary creek bed.
Would the sound of buds breaking
through the thawing earth
change the course of today's
brief-and-endless history?

Who will I be tomorrow
because of the shape of today?

April 12, 1998

On Easter Sunday,
my three-year-old sister steps
in a rabbit's nest.

Holy Uproar from the side yard—
bunnies squeaking, sister squeaking:
harmony of mutual terror.

My brother and I wolf vanilla ice cream
and lamb-shaped cake,
marveling that any mother

would birth her young in our tiered lawn
feet from the drop to the dog's pen,
too young to see our mother crying

—elbows deep in dish suds—
as our father listens to Celtic hymns,
bagpipe and fife.

Waking next morning,
we find three silky pilgrims,
tiny-eared and broken:

little lemmings
too young to know
they had reached the edge of a cliff.

Ticklish

Spring is a lovely, green thing,
sweet sapped and violet covered,
a jubilant shout of vitality
to push back the frost and watery sun,
but I just discovered a tick
crawling on my arm,
and, to be frank,
I don't see the point
of venturing outside any time soon
as I'll be spending the next two days
chasing phantom itches
and jumping when I catch
a freckle out of the corner of my eye.

Love Me Anyway

Conventional wisdom sagely states that
love sees with rose-colored glasses.
But when your eyes meet mine,
they are clear,
no rheumy, soft-focus cinema.
You see me as I am—
my imperfections
my foibles
my faults and flaws—
and you choose to love me anyway.

Good Intentions

Anger, that carry-all
for fear, loneliness, and unmet wanting,
parts my lips and spills to earth,
hot and uncontrolled as bile.
Already, regret coats my mouth,
and I press my teeth together,
a fence of bone
erected too late.

I'm sorry, I say,
I didn't mean it.

But I remember
filling a paper bag
with tender bulbs
at the end summer,
squirreling away
the last hints of sun
for a warmer day.
Today, I found them,
not in the safety of my
cool, dark basement,
but in the breezeway,

where the air is fickle.
Heart sinking,
I pressed a finger to the soggy bulbs,
their life drained away
by sub-zero temperatures
they were never meant to endure,
because my best intentions
can only ever take me
as far as my feet do.

Insecure

He tells her he loves her body
because it's hers,
that the purple-silver lines on her belly
and the way her curves have bled together
don't turn him off.

She doesn't believe him
because she still scans the forms
in every room she walks into,
measuring herself,
weighing her worth
on whether hers is the biggest waist.

She doesn't believe he can love her,
because she has no path to loving herself.

Things I don't let myself enjoy because I feel I didn't earn them enough

The masters diploma hanging on my wall—
    I didn't ace every class,
        so it doesn't count.
The strength of my bones and muscles—
    they're covered in a socially unacceptable
        layer of fat, so it doesn't count.
My children's unquestioning affection—
    they don't yet see the ways I let them down,
        so it doesn't count.
Five quiet minutes of rest for my brain and body—
    I have too much left on my to-do list,
        so it doesn't count.

Today we moved the chickens

Their old coop was drafty
(dilapidated,
shitty)
and their habit of fence hopping
and digging in mulch
digs them in deeper trouble
with the neighbors,
so a new coop was needed.

As thrift is the vogue of the self-employed,
and hinges and lumber
don't grow on trees,
we cannibalized
the drafty-dilapidated-shitty
to finish the cozy-sturdy-clean.

But when the sun set
on the new six-foot hop-less fence,
they shunned the new coop

> (sweet with straw,
> six wings across
> and more

        preening
        perching
        pecking
        space to spare)

and paced the perimeter,
staring at their old roost
    doorless, roofless, hinge-less—
habit winning,
willing to bear the wind
and other elements
as long as they didn't
have to change.

Mother's Day

She brought in her own bouquet:
three fresh peonies from the yard,
a pink so deep it's nearly red,
one soft bloom for each of her own
tender chicks.

Sundays are hard, full
of obligation and standing plans,
not a day to reflect and celebrate
the ones who birthed
(or nursed or cared or comforted)
us. Or, perhaps, it's the only day,
a day when we're either over-shadowed
or over-enshrined—once
and get it over with
until next year. Tomorrow,
busy-ness as usual.

So, she brought in her own bouquet,
and smiled, and celebrated
herself.

Social Anxiety

Yesterday,
while chatting with my friends
on our preferred texting app,
quips hurtling through space and time
from the open plains of Illinois
to a tiny Parisian flat,
spanning the miles between us
faster than thought,
I was suddenly overwhelmed
with the obvious fact
that they all hate me.

Sure I'd put my foot in my mouth,
I closed my phone,
mulling over the faux pas of being me
and how nobody else had made that mistake.
I teetered on the edge of a spiral,
peered down a curling path
I've walked many times before,
but reluctantly turned away
to begin preparing dinner
instead.

Turns out I was only hungry.

After the Phone Call

Perhaps adulthood
is realizing no one escapes
this moment: sitting on the floor
(or the couch, or a bed)
or standing by the window,
phone pressed to my heart
as though I'm holding closed
a chest wound
while my world cants
irreparably
on its axis.
The sensation: the same
syrupy slow-mo
of rolling the truck
on Memorial Day
two decades ago,
my body loose
and floating unrestrained
through the cab,
watching—as if this
is happening to someone else—
as ground
becomes air

becomes sky
and back,
my arms and legs
braced against the roof
and floor, waiting to see
which new way
is up.

Blocked

I have no poetry in me today.
My minutes filled with busy,
strung along like laundry on a line—
the shape of production
but no body to fill them—
I had no time for still,
the thoughtful,
mindful presence one needs
to string words like pearls,
each comma a knot
on a thread
of thought.

To write poetry,
one must live it first.

Better than caffeine

Until you've tried to
bandage an injured chicken
in the middle of

your kitchen on a
Wednesday morning, as her wings
beat against your chest,

have you lived? Have you
truly woken? Nothing quite
stirs the blood so well.

Beach-wise

1.
The first day at the beach,
I scoured the sand, pacing for miles,
hungry to find something

in which to carry away my memories
like a scrap of paper
I could origami and tuck

into the spiraling staircase of a conch shell
or a moon snail's once loved home,
as though the sea owed me anything.

2.
On my second day at the beach,
I loosened my grasp,
the need to control
slipping through my fingers
like so many grains of sand.

I wandered,
but my eyes roved less greedily,
the insatiable hunger to clutch less sharp,

edges dulled by the rolling waves,
my mind a sea-green chip of glass:
no longer useful because of what it can hold
but the beauty it is
all on its own.

3.
The third day I settled,
a wave receding
to the ocean floor,
content simply
to slide across the sand,
unconscious of time,
my fingers loose
and empty.

Ravenous

Yesterday, I learned that
sea otters need to eat
a quarter of their weight
every day—
kelp and clams,
mussels and sea stars—
to survive their harsh life
in frigid oceans,
and I nodded in understanding
for I, too, must consume
a quarter of my brain power
every day—
articles and art,
puzzles and books—
to survive my life
in a broken world.

One marriage ends every 36 seconds

I see this sentence in a list of facts
about divorce in America,
bullet points with no emotion
that I read purely from curiosity

but that leave me counting minutes.
Every wedding is a declaration
—not just of love, fidelity, and partnership,
but a voice of optimism:

we will not be in *that* fifty percent.
Then days become weeks become months
become years of choosing each other
over and over—every 36 seconds.

Perhaps, sometimes, decision fatigue is inevitable.

Demodex

It sounds like something from a horror movie
—arachnids living in the pores of your face—
but NPR assures me it's true.
Clinging fast to the peach fuzz of billions of people,
virtually none of us exist uncolonized.
I rush to the mirror, bending close, eyes crossing,
scouring my face for any sign that I am not alone.

Tilting my head back and forth,
I ponder: is my chin a city?
My upper lip the suburbs?
Do tiny farmers harvest the oil
from the plains of my cheeks
to feed their children?

Passed down by our mothers through
kiss and cuddle, our ancestry can be traced
through a forest of follicles,
our origins mirrored in the DNA
of these microscopic migrants,

which makes me wonder,
do my German mites

and my Swedish mites get along?
Did my Irish mites help build
a transcontinental railroad
from ear to shining ear?
And when I married,
did my mate's mites gaze up in wonder
at the Statue of Liberty
—the loan black hair that insists
on sprouting under my chin—
as they stood in line at immigration?

I picture them, traveling west
to settle in the Rocky Mountain hills of my nose,
their many-faceted eyes shining
with dreams of a better life.

Positive Reinforcement

Months ago
you gave me a picture you'd drawn
of a hummingbird—
your favorite subject for a season,
the one that followed the endless stream
of perfectly arched rainbows,
their vibrant colors reaching from one horizon
to the next—

and, your cheeks pink,
you hungrily scanned my face
for the appropriate reaction.
I must have given a satisfactory answer,
because you skipped away,
on to the next thing
(chasing chickens or
harassing your younger siblings),
and I filed the painting in the stack of paper
too precious to toss but
without a true home.

You've moved on to new subjects,
but you keep filling pages

with birds
and flowers
and friends,
many of whom now also live in that stack
on my desk.

Tonight, you coax me into letting you paint
the fence with me,
even citing that story you're sure you heard
about a boy with a fence to paint
though you can't quite remember who he was
or who wrote the story,
and I quietly smile
and tell you about Samuel Clemens
while we whitewash our way to dusk.

I love painting,
you say,
because I'm an artist,

and I'm staggered by the flippant
comfortable way you take on that mantle—
never doubting, just being—
when it took me decades to finally say that
I'm a writer,
but after I'm done writing these lines,
faltering and frail,

but stronger every time,
I'll trot to your father,
my cheeks pink,
my eyes hungry,
and scan his face.
I love it, he'll say,
and I'll write on.

Annoyance

I love you
but the way you're packaging
the Costco beef
with agonizing care
breaking the log down
piece by piece
and weighing them on the scale
—not a gram out of place—
is setting my teeth on edge.

PMS

I am an over-ripe peach:
easily bruised and weeping
from one small cut—
a single jostle
against hard truth
spilling juicy tears.
The stone in my belly
feels like the whole world,
all there is of me,
nothing to give except
pitted, ugly,
unpalatable,
forgetting that
growth only comes
from the hard parts.

Upon seeing my children's shoes on the floor

The clutter of our home,
the detritus of five people
milling through 1250 square feet
—plus basement—
sometimes makes me flee to the forest.

Not in a metaphorical sense,
or in the "if you don't clean this now
I'm going to run off
and become a wood witch" way,

but physically, literally, following my feet
to that quiet, breathing space
where I can ignore our mundane chaos
and noise, where those

damn shoes
and building blocks,
breakfast crumbs
and mystery socks
can't taunt me.

Here, I don't feel pressured
to launder the blanket of moss
or sort last year's leaves into tidy stacks
or organize the wild violets into a more
aesthetic arrangement
because here, instead of clutter,
I see beauty. Here, I accept the creature-wild,
the being and the letting be,
and I rest.

Be Water

Do not think that you must change the world, darling,
in a burst of furious action,
blowing the norms to smithereens.

Far better to be a drop of water
in a steady stream of other drops
shaping stone over time.

How beautiful the gentle curve,
the sibilant path,
the forest spring carves.

Be slow, steady, soothing,
a single voice among many.
Speak truth with grace.

In a world screaming for dynamite,
be water.

Wednesday Evening, 7:34pm

Bees hum velvet wings,
pollen pantaloons bulging
as they glide along

the clover path that
curls between the garden beds.
I watch, lips parted,

captivated by
these tiny chefs intent on
their work, all the while

flitting through my yard
with sharpened daggers on their
furry little butts.

Remember: "gentle"
is only real when it's strength
made weak on purpose.

Writing Sprint

The hand on my visual timer
slides away, the green pizza slice
growing smaller with each passing second,
and I watch it, fingers poised above my keyboard,
willing a poem to appear. If you look
closely enough, you may even see the faint outline
of a lightbulb above my head,
waiting for illumination.

Billy Collins Envy

the best poetry
feels easy—
the thoughtless
thoughtful
pull and push
of words across the surface
of a mind at play.
artlessly effortless
on the surface,
tricking you into thinking
the poet jotted the words down
in a quick five minutes
at a round metal table
outside a café in Paris
on the back of a napkin
that still bears the evidence of
sipping coffee with too much au lait
—look! a few croissant crumbs
cling to the edge,
and he sweeps them away
to make room
for his final
witty
line.

News Cycle

"There are a lot of kids with guns in Memphis,"
you say with shake of head.
"Where are the parents?"

The story a foot note:
boy injured, 3 a.m.

We grimace,
our eyes captured
only until they slide
to the next story,

the boy and his gun
forgotten

like a strand of spider silk
when the sun slides away—
still floating in the air
but invisible.

Eldest Daughter Syndrome

The masks I wear
change with the setting,
mimicking, reflecting,
built-to-suit.

I'm full of yes
and pleasantly familiar—
the listening ear,
the affirming voice.
I'll drop what I'm doing to
prop you up
in your moment of need.

In kitchens and churches,
on therapist's couches,
sitting on curbs or
walking in the woods,
clutching cups of coffee
or sharing furtive cigarettes,
I'll be what you want,
what you expect to see.

Of course you like me;
I'm you.

This is a poem about overthinking

We have a broody hen in the coop this week,
sitting on a clutch of empty eggs,
no cells dividing and expanding into
more chickens. Still, she sits

and ruffles her feathers and attitude at anyone
boorish enough to prod questing fingers beneath her.
I giggle as she chitters, laugh at her treble growl
over her hoarded vanity, and collect her eggs

despite her protestations. With nothing to protect,
she ventures back into the world, her equilibrium
restored. I wonder if she sees the world with new eyes,
if she regrets the hours she spent dwelling

on something that felt important
but wasn't.

Directions

after Billy Collins

First, head down the flagstone steps
that lead past the goat pens.
I recommend stopping to scratch the tops
of their cow-licked heads;
feel the coarse, stiff hair on your fingertips and
stare for a moment into their
uncanny, sideways eyes
before you march through the ditch
and across the steep gravel drive.

From there, wade through the field of alfalfa
and let its heady aroma tickle your nose
just short of a sneeze,
down through to the garden patch
now florid with late summer produce,
the tomato leaves curling,
and tiptoe into the woods.

A few steps will take you to the creek,
the gravel verge that bit your hand when
you slipped on the ice only
a couple decades ago.

See? The pin-prick scar, white on pink,
still in your palm? You scuffed your chin, too,
when you lost your footing here.
But don't linger; there's more to see.

Follow the current upstream,
facing west and wading—
through weeds or water,
I don't mind which—
around the bend, and another,
past the sheer crags of creek bed
wired together with roots and rock,
until you find Mermaid Lagoon
with its two inevitable stony perches,
twin seats overlooking the flow.

Choose one, and sit.

Observe the way the light shifts
from green to yellow
and back again;
how the cicadas and frogs sing
of love and survival;
how much smaller this space feels
now that you're grown;
how much smaller *you* feel
now that you've seen more of life.

Lame Duck

based on true events

My heart sinks at the sight
of a pure white, domestic duck
feebly flapping her bloodied wings
by the side of the highway.
I tap my brakes, my mind racing—
> Do I stop?
> Where would I take her?
> Who tends to lame ducks?
> How badly is she hurt?

My van pulls abreast of her,
and I crane my neck as we glide past,
clucking my tongue as the duck
transforms into a pure white
grocery sack, red letters telling me
"Thanks for Shopping."

How I hurt my own feelings today:

We sorted the baby clothes this afternoon,
the next step in organizing our home
to reflect the current shape or our lives.

As I tucked away the onesies and hand-knitted
    bonnets in a bin,
I smiled, already picturing our grandchildren
    wearing your clothes
just as they will wear your smile,
and my eyes, and your father's nose.

The longer I held them, though, the murkier my
    memories became,
the past a milk-drenched haze. I wondered
how I could have misplaced the years since
your clothes spanned the length of my forearm—
to now, when I can lean my cheek on the top of your
    head without hunching.

By the Creek

By the creek,
my ample rear-end parked
like a fur seal on the sand,
I watch the lithe bodies of
approximately a million children
splashing in the cold spring water.
Around me sit the other mothers
watching the children
just as I am,
their own asses planted
on the creek bank,
and I marvel at us:
    round, soft bellies
    crinkled eye-corners
    tinseled hair.
How beautifully the years weigh on us
as we watch. Perhaps, like me,
they are remembering with fond awe
how only yesterday
our own lithe bodies
splashed through life,
invigorated
by the cold, crisp water
of youth.

Small Talk

I'm full of words
but none of them pretty
    (disgust
    sputum
    moist
    decay).

I'm tired of perfumed language,
the facade of "I'm fine; how are you?"
when the truth is more nuanced:

I'm earth, full of bones and worms,
belching methane
from my ruminations,
churning the putrid
into something beautiful so that
—yes—
flowers can bloom
but not first, not even most important.

To the man I never write poetry for

Lying together in two-week sheets,
you tell me my breasts smell like fabric softener
and other tantalizing inspirations.

I want to tell you how much I love you,
but there's no room in poetry for another love song
so I will simply tell the truth:

We are an amalgamation of firsts,
holding hands, kissing—
surrounded by trees and grass
and early autumn—
you, so nervous you trembled;
me, so nervous I locked my knees
and luxuriously fainted.
I woke to your furrowed brow
and gentle support.

This is how I think of you:
lifting me over thistles and mud,
disregarding time for my sake,
just like you left your watch in the grass
at the park where you caught me
before I fell.

Graffiti

Outrage, liquid and acidic,
bites me as we brush between
the shear rocks
bordering the creek.

Who felt the need,
the prerogative,
to indelibly mar
this ageless stone?
Why should we care
that Stephie was here
or Hank loved Molly
in the summer of '94?
This is no yearbook
or gas-station toilet stall.

How
dare
they?

Perhaps,
whispers Understanding,

a gentle hand
on my injured sensibilities,
faced with
a place so old and holy,
their mortality
and finitude
grabbed their chin
and said,
    "Look at me."
And so they screamed rebellion
into the void:
    "I am here! I matter!"

Perhaps,
when all is said and done,
this is what we all do,
whether carved in rock
or scribbled on paper;
we leave our mark
however we can,
praying memories of us will fade
as slowly as water erodes
a riverbed.

Thing of Beauty

One orchid blossom
unfurling its freckled face,
awaiting its siblings.

Speckled brown egg,
plucked fresh from sweet straw.

Three stolen minutes
alone
in the sun.

Your smile about nothing
and everything,
a quiet gift
for no one
but me.

Closing House

In the wake of the funeral,
wrung out by the electric storm
of sorrow and condolences,
we wander the house,
realizing its contents are ours now
 —the collective—not *hers*. Not *theirs*.

I imagine their young, elastic faces,
radiant, with decades of hope
stashed in their cheeks like squirrels,
picking the china, the linens, the sturdy hutch.
Now, as we unspool the final threads of their lives,
I see significance in what they chose to bring
from house to house,
from life to life.
They planned their dotage with care:
so little remains
for us to sort and sell.

My feet shush through the carpet,
hands aimlessly opening and closing closets,
and everything has sudden meaning
 —his ties, her resin figurines,

that yesterday only looked like *stuff*.
I long to snatch it up,
ladle it into an apron
gathered at the corners,
leave not a crumb behind
for a mouse who couldn't possibly
know they're dining on memories.

Busy

Today darted like a rabbit,
zigzagging across the hours,
leaving a path of unfinished tasks
strewn in its wake.
Poetry (like the laundry,
and the mending,
and the grout in need of scrubbing)
did not rise to the top of the list
—and won't
if I do not set myself down
carefully
in my chair
ignoring the minutes ricocheting
off the hardwood floor,
and slow myself
long enough to hear
the gentle tapping in my soul:
words, ready to tiptoe out
if they can get through edgewise.

Middle Ages

My Grandma used to say
"Growing old isn't for the faint of heart,"
but I didn't understand what she meant
until today
when I threw my neck out
yawning.

This is a poem about body image

I never pictured myself in a ranch house
with hollow-core doors
and a unibrow roof line,
and I still sometimes fight the urge to compare
my own utilitarian dwelling
to the country cottage of my dreams.
Not until I began to accept this place
for what it is—cozy,
useful, and comfortably familiar—
did I begin to love it, to want to care for it,
to lean into what it is, instead of longing
for what it isn't,
to turn this plain-jane ranch,
into a home.

Reliquary

Looking for my keys,
I plunge my hand into the pocket
of my small green backpack

the purse-sized one I wear on my
three-block meander to the church
where I work and worship

but instead of keys, my fingers find
the round, comforting edges
of an acorn.

In wonder, I pull it out,
wracking my brain for when and where
this hitchhiker joined me.

A memory surfaces
like the last rings of a ripple, faint and slow:
my small son slipping his hand in mine

as he does so often these days,
eschewing the fast pace of his
long-limbed sisters, choosing

to stay with me as we walk.
He smiles up at me,
all freckles and sun,

then solemnly extends
his palm for inspection.
In its center, a perfect acorn,

the same earnest color as his eyes.
I accept his offering,
his implicit adoration,

and he skips ahead,
charging off into the unknown.
Unwitting of its talismanic power,

I reach back and drop
the acorn into my backpack,
ready to sprout

into this moment, distilled,
when I plunge my hand into the pocket,
looking for my keys.

Willms Road

October stings my nostrils:
the scent of harvest, skunk,
and smoldering leaves
heavy with dust and recent twilight.

Gravel crunches patiently underfoot,
monologuing in earthy tones
on sediment and sand.

Brittle air pinches my cheeks
and the gentle roundness of your ears
until they blush from the attention,
red as summer, cold as frost.

Acknowledgements

No act of creativity is complete until shared, so thank you to you, the reader, for picking up this book and sticking around all the way to the acknowledgments page.

I could never have had the confidence (or know-how) to bring this book into the world without my book doulas, my wonderful friends from Moms Who Write. Thank you to Allie, Allison, Amber, Brigid, Emily, Jill, Sarah, Shell, and Tristan for your endless enthusiasm, patience, and feedback.

Many thanks to Cricket, my most faithful (and furry) writing partner. If you could please stop stepping on the keyboard, though, that would be great. I'm going to blame any remaining typos on your feet.

Thank you to Ben, my first reader and biggest cheerleader. You rock, even when you package beef weird.

Credits

These pieces first appeared in the following publications:

"Going Through the Motions" *The Order of Us*, Moms Who Write, April 2022

"Some Days Are Sandstone" Humana Obscura, issue 8, Spring 2024

"Eldest Daughter Syndrome" and "Thing of Beauty" *The Magic of Us,* Moms Who Write, November 2023.

Other poems (in part or in whole) have also appeared on Abby's social media accounts. Find links to those accounts on her website, abbyharding.com/links

About the Author

Abby Harding writes from her home in a small farm town in central Illinois. Her work draws on the natural world, focusing on the intersection of grief and hope. When she's not writing or gazing into the middle distance, she and her husband homeschool their three children and care for a small menagerie of animals (three chickens, two geriatric cats, and a guinea pig named Moose). *Some Days Are Sandstone* is her first poetry collection.

Learn more by scanning the QR code or visiting abbyharding.com

Milton Keynes UK
Ingram Content Group UK Ltd.
UKHW040818121024
449407UK00027B/228/J